YOUR KNOWLEDGE HAS VALUE

- We will publish your bachelor's and master's thesis, essays and papers

- Your own eBook and book - sold worldwide in all relevant shops

- Earn money with each sale

Upload your text at www.GRIN.com and publish for free

Kanchanah Monoharan, Zulkefli Bin Mansor

Review on Project Quality Management Planning

Software Quality Planning

GRIN Publishing

Imprint:

Copyright © 2012 GRIN Verlag GmbH
Print and binding: Books on Demand GmbH, Norderstedt Germany
ISBN: 978-3-656-92843-0

REVIEW ON PROJECT QUALITY MANAGEMENT PLANNING

by

Kanchanah Monoharan Masters in IT, & Dr. Zulkefli Bin Mansor,

Faculty of Computer Science and Information Technology

Universiti Selangor, Malaysia

ABSTRACT

Software Quality Planning is one of the primary processes in Project Quality Management among Quality Assurance and Quality Control. It is an essential practice to deliver a defect free or non-critical bug application that meets client's expectation. The purpose of this research was to find out quality planning failure factors in IT projects. Another aim was to determine, a proper quality planning standard framework that should be implemented in Information Technology (IT) projects. This study examined the earlier researches in quality management and project management areas to identify the failure reasons and critical quality planning dimensions that should be followed in IT projects. Research discovered that there were total 21 vital dimensions plus an additional dimension was introduced in this study. As a conclusion, it is important to have all this elements as a standard in each IT projects to overcome or reduce the number of failures.

Introduction

A project is a temporary endeavour undertaken to create a unique product, service or result. The key to this definition are (Samuel, 2007). IT project is firmly established in the language of business, yet it appears very hard to classify. IT output defined as a piece taking the shape either of software or computing infrastructure (Smyrk, 2007).

A daily routine work performed which falls under two categories operations or projects. Both operations and projects have similar characteristics like individuals carry out the activities, constrained by resources; objectives are planned, executed and controlled.

The differences between these are; operations always referred to repetitive and in progress task whereas project is a temporary venture (specific start and clear end date) to create a unique (different in some distinguishing way) from all other products or services (Choudhuri, 2005).

Overview of Project Management (PM)

PM is the process by which projects are defined, planned, organized, secured, monitored, controlled, delivered and managing resources to achieve specific goals (Alam, 2010).

It is the application of knowledge, skills, tools and techniques to scheme activities to meet project requirements. Sometimes organizations describe PM as an approach to manage ongoing operations to apply PM techniques to them (Choudhuri, 2005). PM is accomplished through the use of the following 5 processes which are initiating, planning, executing, monitoring and controlling and closing.

A good and useful framework provided by the Project Management Institute (PMI). This context breaks down PM into nine management areas (Turbit, 2007). Below are the descriptions of the nine knowledge areas:

i.   Integration Management
ii.   Scope Management
iii.   Time Management

iv.   Cost Management

v.   Quality Management

vi.   Human Resource Management

vii.   Communications Management

viii.   Risk Management

ix.   Procurement Management

In project execution or management, the project team can achieve better project result and job satisfaction by integrating all the 9 knowledge area elements in PM into daily management practice (Eric, 2009). All project managers knew the complication involved in managing a project with a particular group such as a division, an office or even across the organization (Klatch, 2005).

In fact researches constantly show that firms have trouble with IT projects to deliver on time or on budget (Lagerström et al., 2012). Moreover, several projects are cancelled before completion or implementation (Al Neimat, 2005). In a number of cases QM is one of the process researchers fail. A strong QM in a project, it would prevent or minimize few issues (Turbit. 2009).

It is significant to recognize which activities in PM are determinant to the project success to give attention on the management efforts (Marcia et al., 2009).

IT Project Failure Factors

The project team or management will always provide reasons for project failures but the most common causes for project failure are rooted in the project QM process itself and the aligning of IT with organizational cultures (Tilmann and Weinberger, 2004).

Coverdale Organization conducted out a research where the respondents identified estimation mistakes, uncertain project goals and project objectives changing in the middle of the project are key factors in project failures (Neimat,

2005). The subsequent list the main causes for the failure of complex IT projects;

i.   Poor planning

Many of IT projects are planned earlier but that is not enough because it has major milestones and the work prolong throughout each milestone (Humphrey, 2005). Moreover, poor quality planning also leads to late delivery or deadline overdue.

ii.   Unclear goals and objectives

Sometimes poor requirement gathering in the initiation stage of the project will lead to unclear or partially clear goals and objectives (Glaser, 2004; Lagerström et al., 2012). This becomes an issue in quality phase as system or application might not tally with client's aspiration (Baggen et al., 2012).

iii.   Objectives changing during the project

Many project managers might not be aware that a growing or complex IT project (Al Neimat, 2005) will eventually has different objectives which need to be taken care of. Software quality is difficult to maintain when the objectives keep changing in the middle therefore it is recommended to get a sign off from clients before starting the quality planning (Barney et al., 2008).

iv.   Unrealistic time or resource estimates

Common setback during the formation of the Work Breakdown Structure (WBS) is assuming that the time on task equals duration (Lagerström et al., 2012). Time on task represents period taken for the job to complete without any interruptions where else duration counts time of interruptions as well (Al Neimat, 2005). Sometimes when more critical defects are discovered in quality phase, development team might need more time to fix the bugs.

v. **Lack of executive support and user involvement in quality testing**

None in the company feels committed to the project without user participation. Only the end users can test the system from business angle. Besides, management support is vital to set priorities apparent to the employees (Faisal et al., 2010). Team members are usually quite tight with their daily schedules which make them unable to find time to document each and every detail (Al Neimat, 2005).

vi. **Failure to communicate and act as a team**

Since IT projects are complex, employees are always busy with task and analysis which reduces the teamwork. Project managers do not communicate so often to increase the bonding between team members because they believe it might affect their progress or productivity (Glaser, 2004). This communication breakdown affects in knowledge sharing of the application which is stressed in this research on quality planning process (Faisal et al., 2010).

vii. **Inappropriate skills**

Once the project starts to grow, the requirement for resources increases too with superb planning, creativity, good communication skills, functional or tools experience which is not necessary to find in an individual (Glaser, 2004; Poon et al., 2012). Quality tools are also upgrading and some are required to replace with new one according to market trend or client requirement (Mäntylä et al., 2012).

Therefore, in this paper project QM will be focused as it is the most important area in current IT world.

Overview of QM

The word quality originates from the Latin word quails meaning 'what kind of'. In the midst of a diversity meaning and implications, it is referred to as a 'slippery concept' (Pfeffer and Coote, 1991).

Quality can be categorized into good and poor quality. Good quality will always increase the productivity, high cost effectiveness, high customer satisfaction and minimize the risk. Where else poor quality increases risk, low ethical, decrease in productivity and bad in customer satisfaction (Lalita, 2008; Bijlsma et al., 2012).

Quality revolution or QM movement begins from these important "gurus", W. Edwards Deming, Walter A. Shewhart, Joseph M. Juran, Philip B. Crosby and Kaoru Ishikawa (Crocker, 2003). Shewart developed the Plan-Do-Check-Act (PDCA) cycle as well as theories of statistical process control and the Shewart Transformation Process (Anderson, 2009; Wiedemann, 2009).

Research shows that Walter A. Shewart's work might be used by Deming and Juran after the World War II to ascertain the quality process (Crocker, 2003). In addition, Joseph M. Juran defined quality as 'fitness for purpose' (Mishra, 2007). He developed the quality trilogies which are quality planning, improvement and control. QM plans for quality enhancements that raise the level of performance (Anderson, 2009).

Juran also recommends team work and introduced ten stages of approaches to quality improvement (Mishra, 2007). Besides, W. Edwards Deming is recognized as the father of quality movement (Mishra, 2007). He developed the "fourteen points" and "seven deadly diseases of management" a total philosophy of management. Basically he improved the findings by Shewhart with his explanations of variation, use of control charts and theories on knowledge and psychology. Besides, he helped to popularize the PDCA cycle by focusing on QM, which eventually became "Deming Cycle" (Anderson, 2009).

Moreover, Philip B. Crosby is probably the most influential management thinker in United States and Europe (Mishra, 2007). He developed two ideas "quality is free" and "zero defects". Crosby's ideas emphasize that implementing quality improvement by eliminating all defects or minimizing it to an acceptable quality level will increase the revenue from greater customer (Anderson, 2009). Crosby is famous for his four absolutes of QM (Crosby, 1984);

   i.   The meaning of quality is conformance to customer requests.

   ii.   The end product to reach quality is prevention and not detection.

   iii.   The standard of performance is zero defects.

   iv.   The measurement of quality is the value of non-conformance.

There were many people in Japan who made contributions in quality but this guru Kaoru Ishikawa is the best known in North America. He developed the Ishikawa diagram and also well known for introduced the seven basic tools of quality and the philosophy of total quality (Anderson, 2009).

There are numerous business processes in an organization depending on their internal or external software. These software applications are very important for the success of the organization. Nevertheless, the failure rate for software projects remains high and many IT projects have unsatisfactory end products (Keil et al., 2002). Project QM knowledge area of PM which activities make sure that the project will satisfy the client needs for what it was produced.

Traditional Against Modern QM

In traditional QM (Alexandros and Constantinos, 2007) practices each department required to take care of their own issues. They do not discuss with other teams to find out where is the root cause of the problem. Besides, this traditional concept just has single inspection point (Michael and Marina, 2003) which allows only the end product to undergo the quality check point. These activities increase the chances of rework or scrap which eventually expands the cost of the project.

Where else in modern QM (Alexandros and Constantinos, 2007) context they do not follow the departmentalized approach but the whole organization required to be concerned about quality improvement. In this respect, cross-functional work teams are encouraged which will ultimately deal with inter-departmental management issues (Mäntylä et al., 2012). Therefore, more attentions (Michael and Marina, 2003) are given to the human aspect in terms of the processes, approach to quality and the concept of TQM (Carroll, 1995). This modern concept is more oriented towards process improvements through multiple inspection points. One of the key changes can be noticed is that the attitude of everyone is responsible for quality. Multiple quality check point provides space for corrections to be made in the earlier stage before additional work is done which minimizes the cost of rework and scrap.

Thus QM should be emphasize in all phases of a project like throughout the software development life cycle (SDLC), for the reason that if a severe defect is detected at the closure of the project, only miniature actions can be taken to solve the problem (Liu et al., 2006; Wiedemann, 2009). Hence, QM is not something that is applied at one stage but have to be a continuous process (Balla et al., 2002).

Project QM Process

QM process consists of quality planning, quality assurance and quality control activities of the performing organization that determine quality policies and objectives for the project to satisfy the needs for which it was undertaken (PMBOK, 2008).

The first process, quality planning is done as part of the planning process group, followed by quality assurance which done as part of the executing process group and the final process is quality control which done as part of the monitoring and control process group (Rakesh, 2010)

These processes interact with each other and may engage effort from one or more individuals or teams. Each process takes place at least once in every project and it may overlap.

Dimensions in QM Planning

The objective of the quality planning process is to identify appropriate standard for the success of project execution to achieve the desired quality level. Once the standard is determined, planning activities should be focused on task involves meeting the standard.

A project manager must allocate the task and manage the project team (Rakesh, 2010).

Besides the manager should also improve current processes to minimize the defect area and at the same point save time and cost (Lagerström et al., 2012).

Quality planning is the main or critical process in project QM but usually it will be given the least concentration due to lack of understanding about quality and its integral part in a project.

This element should not be underestimating and organization board must give full support to it by encouraging project team to allocate ample time for quality planning. Managers should be sent for QM workshops from time to time to update their knowledge on the latest quality planning practices utilized in IT organizations.

Defining quality standard in all phases of SDLC is important due to great number of activities present in each stage of it (Wiedemann, 2009). This research will primarily focus on adequate quality planning, as deficiency in planning phase restrains the victory of quality assurance and quality control efforts (Marcia et al., 2009).

There are three elements under quality planning which assists, monitors and controls quality assurance and quality control phases as well. Those are;

i. **Input**

   Requirements and other information to begin quality planning need to be documented.

ii. **Tools & Techniques**

   The methods to execute and monitor quality assurance and quality control phase.

iii. **Output**

   Information that has been captured will be evaluated at end of quality phase.

Figure 1.0 list out all the necessary Inputs, Tools and Techniques and Outputs for QM planning as per PMI standard. A new activity called "Training Schedule" in Input field has been introduced in this research based on the modern QM perception on people aspects.

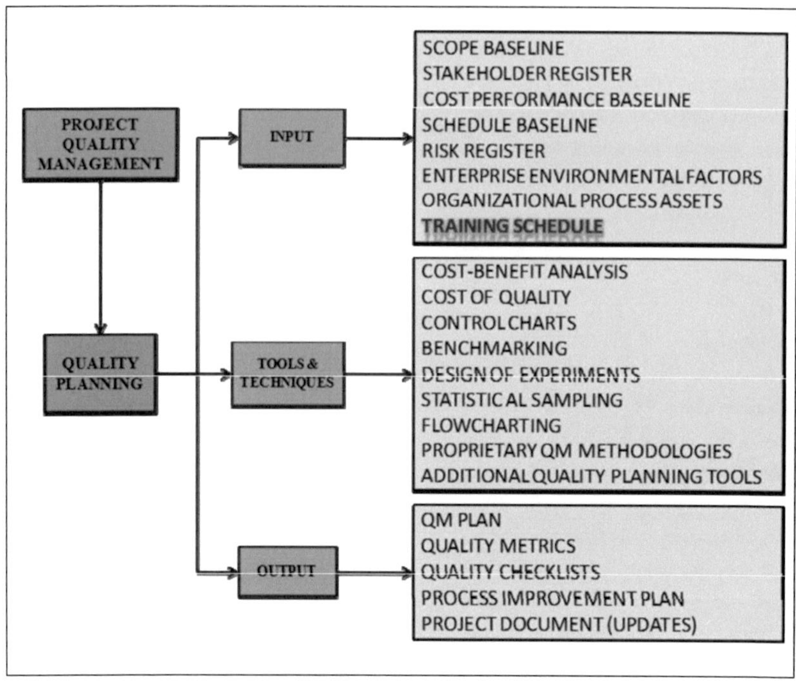

Figure 1.0: Conceptual Framework on QM Planning

Conclusion

As a summary this research identified the possible IT projects failure factors from different angle. The failure factors are identified due to lack of focus in software quality planning phase. Furthermore, this study determined the QM planning standard that should be implemented in IT projects by referring to the existing standard in PMI and PMBOK.

Fundamentally each of the knowledge area is important process that has to be accomplished within its discipline in order to achieve a successful PM. Besides, they also fall into one of the PM process groups, that creates a matrix structure in such a way that every process can be related to one knowledge area and one process group. However the most critical component where project failure occurs is in quality region which is the main reason for choosing this research topic.

Moreover importance is given to people management in modern Project QM aspects, where three sections; plan quality, perform quality assurance and perform quality control play a vital role. Among these three process, quality planning contributes to the success of quality assurance and quality control that ultimately brings triumph to a project in defects prevention.

Therefore, research has been narrowed to quality planning phase that be full of inputs, tools and techniques and outputs based on PMI standard in PMBOK 4th Edition, 2008. New feature skill set upgrading schedule has been introduced by researcher to increase the project or tools knowledge level of the employee with current or future tasks to prevent major defects escaping from tester's eyes in development or testing environment itself.

References

1. A Guide to the Project Management Body of Knowledge (PMBOK @ Guide). (2008). (4th Ed.). Pennsylvania: Project Management Institute (PMI).

2. Al Neimat, T. (2005). *Why IT Projects Fail*. Retrieved from The Project Perfect White Paper Collection.

3. Alam, M. U. (2010). *10 Free Tools for Effective Project Management*. Retrieved January 9, 2012, from http://www.smashingapps.com/2010/02/1 5/10-free-tools-for-effective-project management.html

4. Alexandros, G. P., & Constantinos, V. P. (2007). Understanding Total Quality Management in Context: Qualitative Research on Managers' Awareness of TQM Aspects in the Greek Service Industry. *The Qualitative Report,* 12(1), 40-66.

5. Anderson, C. (2009). *Top Ten Quality Gurus*. RetrievedJ anuary 23, 2012, from http://www.bizmanualz.com/blog/top- ten/top-ten-quality-gurus.html

6. Baggen, R., Correia, J. P., Schill, K., & Visser, J. (2012). Standardized code quality benchmarking for improving software maintainability. *Software Quality Journal,* 20(2), 287-307.

7. Balla, K., Bemelmans, T., Kusters, R., & Trienekens, J. (2002). Quality through Managed Improvement and Measurement (QMIM): Towards a Phased Development and Implementation of a Quality Management System for a Software Company. *Software Quality Journal,* 9(1), 177-193.

8. Barney, S., Aurum, A., & Wohlin, C. (2008). A Product Management Challenge: Creating Software Product Value through Requirements Selection. *Journal of Systems Architecture,* 54(6), 576-593.

9. Bijlsma, D., Ferreira, M. A., Luijten, B., & Visser, J. (2012). Faster issue resolution with higher technical quality of software. *Software Quality Journal,* 20(2), 265-28.

10. Carroll, J. (1995). The application of total quality management to software development. *Information Technology & People,* 8(4), 35–47.

11. Choudhuri, N. M. (2005). *Project Management Fundamentals*. ITC Infotech India Ltd. Retrieved January 1, 2012, from http://www.giorgiogiussani.it/project- managemet_EN.pdf

12. Crocker, O., West, E., & Saravanan, M. (2003). Leadership and Strategic Perspective of Quality Management: An introduction. Retrieved March ?, ?012, from http://www.slideshare.net/edwardycs/quali ty-management-u1

13. Crosby, P. B. (1984). *Quality without tears*. Singapore: McGraw Hill.

14. Eric, T. (2009). *The Dynamics of Project Management*. Retrieved from The Project Perfect White Paper Collection.

15. Faisal, T., Zillur, R., & Qureshi, M. N. (2010). The relationship between total quality management and quality performance in the service industry: a theoretical model. *International Journal of Business, Management and Social Sciences,* 1(1), 113-128.

16. Glaser, J. (2004). *Management's role in IT project failures*. Retrieved February 12, 2012, from Healthcare Financial Management.

17. Humphrey, W. (2005). *Why Big Software Project Fail: The 12 Key Questions*. Retrieved February 14, 2012, from The Journal of Defense Software Engineering.

18. Keil, M., Tiwana, A., & Bush, A. A. (2002). Reconciling user and project manager perceptions of IT project risk: a Delphi study. *Information Systems Journal,* 12(1), 103-119.

19. Klatch, W. (2005). *Running a Supply Chain Project*. Retrieved from The Project Perfect White Paper Collection.

20. Lagerström, R., Würtemberg, L. M., Holm, H., & Luczak, O. (2012). Identifying factors affecting software development cost and productivity. *Software Quality Journal,* 20(2), 395-417.

21. Lalita, J. (2008). *Q&A - Changes in Project Quality Management Chapter*. Retrieved January 1, 2012, from. http://www.scribd.com/doc/6738833/QA-Changes-in-Project-Quality-Management-Chapter

22. Liu, X., Kane, G., & Bambroo, M. (2006). An Intelligent Early Warning System for Software Quality Improvement and Project Management. *The Journal of Systems and Software,* 79(1), 32-38. doi: 10.1109/TAI.2003.1250167.

23. Mäntylä, M., Itkonen, J., & Iivonen, J. (2012). Who tested my software? Testing as an organizationally cross-cutting activity. *Software Quality Journal,* 10(1), 145-172.

24. Marcia, F. L. C., António, M. J. P., & João, E. Q. A. S. V. (2009). Software projects' most important activities of quality management: A Delphi study. *Communications of the IBIMA,* 11(1), 60-66.

25. Michael, W. N., & Marina, N. G. (2003). The *Project Management Question and Answer Book*. New York: American Management Association (AMACOM).

26. Mishra, S. (2007). *Quality Assurance In Higher Education: An Introduction*. India: Commonwealth of Learning; National Assessment and Accreditation Council.

27. Pfeffer, N., & Coote, A. (1991). *Is Quality Good for You? A Critical Review of Quality Assurance in the Welfare Services*. London: Institute of Public Policy Research.

28. Poon, P. L., Tse, T. H., Tang, S. F., & Kuo, F. C. (2012). Contributions of tester experience and a checklist guideline to the identification of categories and choices for software testing. *Software Quality Journal,* 19(1), 141-163.

29. Rakesh, S. (2010). *Project Quality Management Process*. Retrieved February 12, 2012 from Articlesbase.

30. Smyrk, J. (2007). *What does the term "IT project" actually mean? : A challenge to the IT profession*. Retrieved January 30, 2012 from Philica.com.

31. Tilmann, G., & Weinberger, J. (2004). *Technology Never Fails, but Project Can. 1(26)*, 28. Retrieved February 19, 2012, from computer source database at http://www.ebscohost.com.

32. Turbit, N. (2007). *Simple Project Management Explanation.* Retrieved from The Project Perfect White Paper Collection.

33. Turbit, N. (2009). *Project Managing a New Boat.* Retrieved from The Project Perfect White Paper Collection.

34. Wiedemann, A. (2009). Evaluation Methodology for Assessing Management System Establishment Support Tools. *The Open Software Engineering Journal,* 3(1), 9-14.